DIARY

OF

THE REVEREND GEORGE FOX, M.C.

JUNE 16TH 1944 - JUNE 6TH 1945

edited by his son

The Reverend Colin Fox

Published 1998

by

WILTON 65
Flat Top House, Bishop Wilton, York. YO4 1RY

Copyright © Colin Fox

All rights reserved. No part of this publication may be reproduced, stored in a retrieval system or transmitted in any form or by any means without the prior written permission of the publisher, nor be otherwise circulated in any form of binding or cover other than that in which it is published and without a similar condition being imposed on the subsequent purchaser.

ISBN 0 947828 48 6

Printed
in
Great Britain

To all who served in the
3rd Reconnaissance Regiment,
Northumberland Fusiliers,
and to the memory of those
who died in battle.

GEORGE FOX ON HIS ENGAGEMENT TO
MARGARET DAVIDSON - MAY 1942

Stay with me, God. The night is dark.
The night is cold: my little spark
Of courage dies. The night is long:
Be with me, God, and make me strong.

I love a game: I love a fight.
I hate the dark: I love the light.
I love my child: I love my wife.
I am no coward. I love Life.

Life with its change of mood and shade
I want to live. I'm not afraid.
But me and mine are hard to part:
Oh, unknown God, lift up my heart.

You stilled the waters at Dunkirk
And saved Your servants. All Your work
Is Wonderful, dear God. You strode
Before us down that dreadful road.

[*This poem was found amongst George Fox's papers: Entitled* A Soldier - His Prayer, *it was written by a soldier sheltering in a slit trench during the Battle of El Agheila*].

CONTENTS

	Page
Photograph of George Fox	Frontispiece
Poem	
Preface by The Reverend Colin Fox	1
Foreword by Major General Dare Wilson	3
Glossary	5
Map	6
The Diary	7
Recommendation leading to the award of the Military Cross	61
Illustrations of the Military Cross and Territorial Decoration	62
George Fox's letter of 6th June 1944, to his eldest daughter Elizabeth	63-68
Acknowledgements	69
Index	

PREFACE
by
The Reverend Colin Fox

My father was born on 28th July 1912 near Erpingham, Cromer, Norfolk. He went to King Edward VI school in Norwich, followed by St. John's Hall, Cockfosters, which was to become the London College of Divinity, part of the University of London. He qualified as A.L.C.D. in 1936 and was ordained a deacon in September of that year. He served his first curacy at Emmanuel Church, Guildford and moved to Bath in 1938 to begin his second curacy at St. Andrew and St. Swithun, Walcot.

It was while preaching at St. Andrew's, Bath on 3rd September 1939 that a note was passed to him to say that war had been declared.

My father immediately volunteered for military service and in October 1939 he was granted an Emergency Commission as a Chaplain to the Forces, Class IV. He was first attached to the Fifth Royal Inniskilling Dragoon Guards, and in November 1939 went with that unit to France as part of the British Expeditionary Force. He was reported missing, presumed killed, on 4th June 1940. However, he made his own way on foot from Rheims to St. Nazaire, and was able to get back to England by the end of June.

My father was then attached to the 8th Battalion of the Royal Northumberland Fusiliers, which later became the 3rd Reconnaissance Regiment, commanded by Colonel Hugh Merriman, DSO., MC., who later became my Godfather. At the end of 1941 that unit was stationed at Berkhamsted, Hertfordshire, and on New Year's Eve of that year my father met my mother, Margaret Davidson. She was the elder daughter of Viscount and Viscountess Davidson. In 1937 my grandmother had succeeded her husband as Member of Parliament for Hemel Hempstead, when he had become a member of the House of Lords.

My father and mother married on 13th February 1943 at the Savoy Chapel.

My parents' first child, my eldest sister Elizabeth, was born on 21st December 1943. In the preparation for D-Day, on 6th June 1944 my father wrote a letter to Elizabeth, which I have reproduced at the end of this book. He had very much in mind that he might not see my mother or sister again. Ten days later he embarked, and began keeping the diary. He had no thought that it would ever be published.

My father was demobilised in October 1945. His award of the Military Cross was gazetted on 21st January 1946.

At the end of 1945 my father became priest-in-charge of Nettleden with Potten End, Hertfordshire, where I was born and between 1946 and 1950 he was the Vicar of St. Andrew's, Bedford, where my sister Catherine was born.

After the war my father maintained his interest in, and affection for the Army, by serving as a Chaplain with the Territorial Army, first with the Bedfordshire and Hertfordshire Yeomanry and later with the Queen's Royal Rifles until 1964. He was awarded the Territorial Decoration in 1960.

Between 1950 and 1955 my father served as Archdeacon of Cornwall, and Rector of Montego Bay, Jamaica, where my twin sisters Penelope and Rosemary were born in 1953.

He returned in 1956 to become Vicar of St. Etheldreda's, Fulham, which involved taking on the challenge of re-building St. Etheldreda's Church, which had been reduced to a bomb site during the war. He also became Chaplain to the West Indian community in London.

In 1965, on the invitation of the Bishop of Ely, Edward Roberts, who had been Bishop of Kensington, my father took up his final appointment as Archdeacon of Wisbech and Vicar of Haddenham. He also became an Honorary Canon of Ely Cathedral. He died while still holding these appointments on 6th November 1978.

Colin Fox

FOREWORD
by
MAJOR-GENERAL DARE WILSON, C.B.E., M.C.

When writing about a Man of God a layman, particularly if he be a soldier, must watch his step. In the case of George Fox I am happy to accept all the risks save that of failing to do him full justice.

To me George was the ideal Regimental Chaplain. He had all the virtues which soldiers look for in their Padre and many more besides. As all who have served at *the sharp end* know, there are times when, more than anything else, one needs a wise head to turn to, or a shoulder to lean on, be it for advice, understanding or strength. In soldiers' language the Padre has a direct line to God and in times of danger that counts for a lot because, for most of us, the power of prayer does not come easily.

George gave his support whenever and wherever it was needed to thousands of soldiers throughout the war and it was as Chaplain to the 3rd Reconnaissance Regiment, formerly the 8th Battalion Royal Northumberland Fusiliers and therefore comprised mainly of Geordies, that he spent the last 4 years of the war. These were the men for whom he did so much and whose respect and affection he gained, often through his understanding of the importance of being a good listener. His diary covering the last year of the war in North West Europe takes this side of his work for granted and there is very little mention of his never-ending correspondence, much of it dealing with welfare cases and comforting the relatives of casualties, because in many cases he knew more about the men than a recently arrived troop or squadron commander. But the wide scope of his responsibilities is there for the reader to ponder with its harrowing and simply-told accounts of his work in the field. It is a striking revelation of a man of the deepest spiritual convictions and sense of duty constantly working on behalf of the wounded and dying and all too often responsible for the fetching and burial of the dead under the worst possible conditions. Few men with George's sensitivity could have continued facing such traumas without considerable inner strength and I can only conclude that it came from a Divine source. When, for example, he describes *'perhaps one of the most impressive evening services I have ever held'* which he took in a barn with contrived lighting and still half full of straw, concluding *'from the candles on the altar we all worshipped God - God was there and refreshed we went away'*, may be we have the answer.

    We served together and saw much of each other during those eventful years. More than 25 years later while I was still a bachelor I visited him in his parish near Ely to ask his advice concerning the most important step a man can take in life. He encouraged me to take that step and a quarter of a century further on I am still thankful.

January 1997

Glossary of Abbreviations

A.D.S.	Advanced Dressing Station
A.F.V.	Armoured Fighting Vehicle
Bde	Brigade
B.L.A.	British Liberation Army
D.A.A.G.	Deputy Assistant Adjutant General
D.A.C.G.	Deputy Assistant Chaplain General
D.C.G.	Deputy Chaplain General
F.D.S.	Field Dressing Station
H.C.	Holy Communion
L.R.C.	Light Reconnaissance Car
M.O.	Medical Officer
O.P.	Observation Post
O.R's	Other Ranks
R.A.Ch.D.	Royal Army Chaplains Department
R.A.M.C.	Royal Army Medical Corps
R.A.P.	Regimental Aid Post
R.E's	Royal Engineers
R.H.Q.	Regimental Headquarters
S.C.F.	Senior Chaplain to the Forces
S.S. Bde	Special Service Brigade - commandos

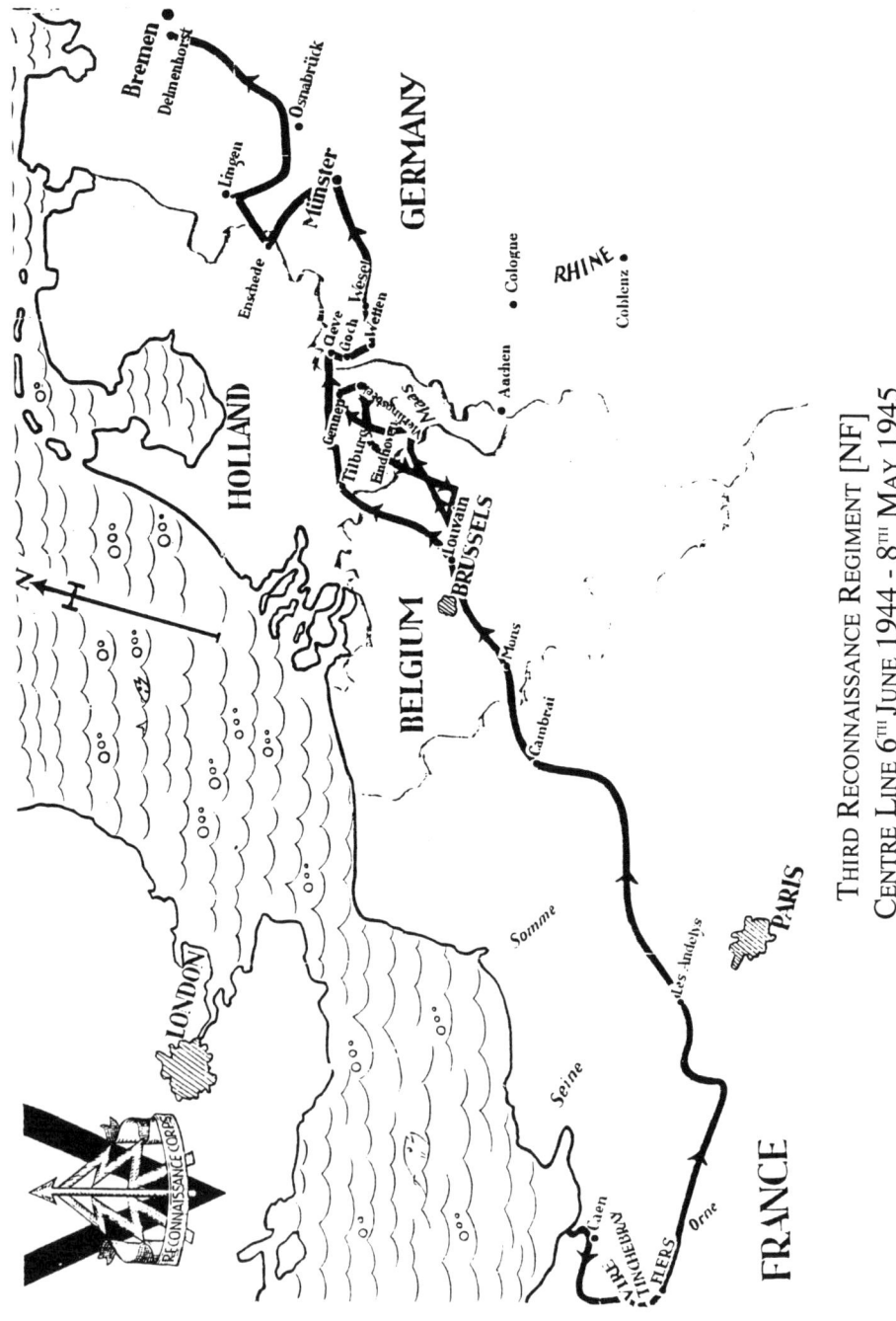

THE DIARY

Note. *The diary is reproduced exactly as it is in the original document except when the meaning was unclear. Any alterations other than to punctuation are shown in bracketed italics within the text or as annotated notes. For convenience, dates are in* **BOLD** *text.*

June 16th 1944 The marshalling areas near Grays were reached without events, a grand day and everyone was on top of their form. As the convoy wended its way through the small village and deviating from the centre of London by the North Circular Route many greetings and wishes were passed by the onlookers and as we passed them, both young and old; one felt an earnestness and affection, their "God bless" and Victory signs were not empty gestures. Others were silent, but with a look of gratitude on their faces; to them the War had come very near, we were going out to see that their son or boyfriend died not in vain. 'A' Sqn. was presented with £29 of money collected throughout a factory for any convoy that stopped outside the factory on its way to France.

The marshalling areas were reached and here everything was well laid on, from vomit bags to delousing shirts. I considered both a necessity. The night was greatly disturbed by remote controlled planes[1], bombs were dropped in the vicinity, but with very little damage. Midday the 16th we left for Tilbury, all went well and facilities were excellent - a sing-song was held on the foc'sle, and to many of the troops nautical life was a novelty; the Cockneys passed numerous wisecracks as they passed Southend and reminisced profusely about good old days.

---

[1] Vl 'Flying Bombs'

I had a good night's sleeping in the captain's cabin on the settee, another officer was at my feet on the floor, the noise of the engines did not disturb my rest.

In the morning I learned that we were still anchored as overnight, awaiting the arrival of another ship. There is a slight swell and a fresh breeze.

The day passed quietly with a sing-song in the mess deck, the spelling Bee and Quiz proved a great success, one rating even went so far as to say that Canada was the capital of America. Towards evening and as we began to sail, the sea became rough, the atrocious feeling of frustration crept upon me, but retiring to bed both stomach and sea settled down.

Sunday was a beautiful day, I held two services, an H.C. in the Ward Room which was a truly representative gathering, both Naval and Army personnel, and a short service was held on the foc'sle; there were a large number of troops present. The remainder of the day passed in 'zizzing' and storing up rest for the future.

Sunday: 2030 hours: Marvellous sight forward, *HMS Nelson* in distance, and all round every type of ship, here is the armed might of Britain, Spitfires came out of the setting sun periodically and one feels proud to travel and take part in such an undertaking. At 2200 hours smoke screen laid and throughout the night intermittent ack ack fire - at 0400 hours the boat began to roll and by 0730 hours a 60 m.p.h. gale was blowing, an attempt at landing was considered but thought inadvisable in view of the rough sea. Troops were bearing up well, a few cases of sickness and time for more sleep, becoming sleep bound if that is possible.

Tuesday. Still at sea, impossible to land for fear of the

ship breaking her back, sleeping and eating is becoming monotonous - no activity whatsoever, an occasional 'crump'. There were numerous alarms about landing, but at last minute advised otherwise. Not actually sick but one's stomach feels out of joint: still more sleep.

24/6/44. Four days of battle inoculations - the first 24 hours seemed like an exercise in the south - shells constantly going overhead or even ack ack fire did not impress it upon one's mind - not until one of our men was killed as a result of shell-fire, and the planning of a Military Funeral in an improvised divisional cemetery, did it all come back again.

25/6/44. Services were held in various areas and all of them were very well attended, no longer is coercion needed, men come and find in things spiritual a consolation, even their wildest dreams in peace time could not have told them that to the Church they would have to turn. Now is the time to impress them, but will the time be too short, in order that their future may be secured?

27/6/44. First time under actual fire, about 1200 yards from enemy lines, number of shells came over and landed near truck - Messerschmitt 109s put in an appearance, but they suddenly realised we had command of the sky and returned to their homes as quickly as they came. After a short time, I found myself having one ear flapping for the sound of the whizzing of a shell, one eye on a trench into which I could dive and the remainder of my powers on the person with whom I was conversing: The men were rather tired and weary after a bad night of rain and being alert for night patrols.

28/6/44. About to move to forward areas. A pleasant day, am writing this beneath an apple tree - all well. Fear that I have lapsed in my writing due to these factors - mainly slackness, and time and frame of mind to unite thoughts.

2/7/44. A busy Sunday, but one which I shall always remember, for while at Periers-sur-le-Dan preparing for a service a shell fell 5½ yards from me, a trooper standing by was killed, died in the ambulance: The whole thing was terrifying, black smoke and flames enveloped me, and threw me down, branch of a tree fell upon me. Never before in my life have I felt death so near - how it missed me no one knows: Thank God. I proceeded with my services with the 2 Mx; at the commencement of the service I warned the men that if a shell should whine overhead, then everyone for himself, in the middle of the Lord's Prayer one was heard, and padre and congregation were horizontal, but that was not the end, for during the last hymn *'Soldiers of Christ arise'* the first line saw sixty robust men fall flat, only to rise again.

My constitution and mental powers were definitely shaken, but there was more work for me to do.

While in Gayelle the Boche shelled regularly and most disconcerting - one evening he 'stonked' savagely, and one trooper in getting into his trench had his brains blown out, it was grim and how difficult to preserve one's sanity and equilibrium and to roam about the field in the midst of it all, the feeling of the next one may be yours and again the words "in the midst of life we are in death" becomes more and more real.

The remainder of that evening was spent in a trench: at 11.30 hours we went to F.D.S. with a patient, an air of complacency and efficiency was over them all. Services were held in the field, and it had to be conducted in two parts, a number of men attended, and they all paid a noticeable attention, there was a feeling pervading amongst them all of a longing for Divine things.

I have just witnessed a wonderful sight, date being 2200 hours: **7/7/44**, of 450 Halifaxes and Lancasters bombing German concentrations north of Caen - it was a thrilling and moving spectacle, but at the same time there were mixed feelings for those who were undergoing such a bombardment - hundreds of our airmen went through the 'flak' nothing stopped them, German 'ack-ack' proved to be ineffective. I could not help thinking of Caen, and its close association with English life and culture, a city with Norman, Gothic and Romanesque architecture, and of course the burial place of William the Conqueror - I hope soon to see its beauties.

At midnight we departed for another area, the roads assumed an eerie outlook, tanks rolled forward - fires were burning in the countryside - yes Caen it was - that architecture and people killed and maimed - my mind wandered freely - shells still whistled overhead, enemy planes tried to penetrate our defences, tracer bullets in multi-colours went slowly skywards to meet the invader - the thought of Brock firework display of peace-time days came back racing through my mind.

At our new harbour we dug a trench, and we dug hard, battling with roots and hard soil to find cover - but no sleep was forthcoming for at 0400 hours hell was let loose. *HMS*

Rodney, *HMS Warspite* and thousands of artillery guns went mad, the earth rocked and so we moved forward - still no sleep - more advances, but no one minds so long as we go on.

By Sunday **7/7/44** the first objectives had been achieved, and our bridgehead has been enlarged, how cramped we had become, and anything that he decided to send over would be sure to hit a vehicle or dump. I visited La Bijude and Epron - just devastated walls only four feet high remain, the place stank to high heaven - the cats roam amongst the debris - dead cows lie here and there and at intervals lie some of our men - beside the grave is an upturned rifle with bayonet keeping it erect - the objective had been attained.

I was informed that some men had been lying in a wood since 'D' day, once 'No Man's Land' - the sight and smell was indescribable, they were of the Warwickshire Regiment - letters and photographs were found in their trench - one letter which had been written only a few minutes before, spoke of planning for the future - they were given a Christian burial in the trench where they fell - God bless their souls - brave men. It is so difficult to get one's mind straight after witnessing such a scene, one cannot conceive that once they were like you. All this is so hateful, it makes all men feel disgusted that civilisation could have fallen so low: I hope that will never fall again to my lot:

The week went well with routine duties - many Holy Communion Services were held, - one in a once magnificent château, glass was scattered over a priceless carpet and pictures slashed - walls riddled with bullets, and amongst it all we knelt and took to ourselves the Bread of Life and so into the world we went - new men.

I met an officer in the R.E's who had visited Caen, and most emphatically he told me that he was ashamed at being an Englishman to see such damage - but I tried to point out that sacrifice in buildings and life had to be made in order that France might be free - and we must hope that nothing further will be seen again.

17/7/44. My morale has been lifted today regarding the coming attack, for I have learned that if it is successful it will be the end of the war - the whole bridgehead is seething with activity.

On the **18th July** at 5.15 the first wave of aircraft roared overhead to bomb German strongpoints, they kept coming with their load without a break for 2½ hours, the early morning freshness was soon turned into the smell of cordite - the factory at Colombelles was clouded in smoke. At 0815 hours our armour rolled into action, we all looked upon this as the great break through, some made wishful statements - but throughout the whole day the battle roared, advances were made and objectives achieved. As I stood on a German Mark IV tank looking towards the battlefield my heart was stirred by the armed might of Britain, but the enthusiastic heart bubble began to subside when I thought of men I know going forward never to return again - but this battle will be the beginning of the end - I wonder?

The day passes quietly waiting for our turn, and come it did. Notice to pack up was short, and to Ouistream the convoy made its way; the roads were blocked with ammunition and supplies and over the river we went - Royal Engineers were repairing one that had been blown - we went in a long line and the noise of battle began to draw near - now and then we would pass German prisoners going back, they looked incredibly scruffy, the O.R's to all outward appearances seemed cowed, but the officers still bore a truculent air.

We entered Escoville later in the evening and had to begin to dig, but owing to the ground being so hard the M.O. and I decided to take to the ditch, but sleep was not to be had owing to vicious attacks by mosquitoes from all directions - not excluding the German bombers who came over in a half-hearted way to retaliate on our previous day's bombing - they dropped anti-personnel bombs but no appreciable damage was done.

In the morning I saw damage done in the village, bodies were lying by the roadside, a terrible sight. I used German trailers to convey bodies to improvised cemetery; one man had had part of his head blown off, and as I got to lift what was left, I pulled my hand away quickly, that feeling had never occurred to me before, it was awful. Two of us lifted that mangled frame into the trailer, and as we pushed it through the smoky and dusty street, German prisoners passed me - how strange it all was, that lad killed him probably, now they were going back to safety - odd thoughts passed through my mind. I could not get things clear - so we trudged on to the graveside; they were given a Christian burial, and into God's hands I committed them.

On Sunday of that week **23/7/44** I had some very realistic services, we knelt and prayed at the altar, we left refreshed to face the world.

On **24/7/44** the R.A.P. was transferred to the cellar of a château in Escoville, and the feeling of security in the midst of that concrete helped matters considerably, but that added sense of security had its repercussions when coming out of that cave, it perhaps was not a good thing. The last night a bomb fell on the steps of the cellar, things clattered down, masonry came crashing - vengeance was truly felt, the Hun was ready to do his worst, we dressed in semi-darkness, got the floor clear for casualties - when things quietened, we ventured out, all was now quiet, but a dark red glow appeared in the sky, a petrol lorry on fire probably, by a miracle no casualties appeared, we retired again the time being now 3 am, but a poor night's sleep it was - in the morning we had packed and were away out of the line, for a rest - I only hope that we shall be able to relax, for relaxation is needed by us all - even back at Colleville shells can be heard whining in the distance falling on St Aulin: Our dug-out I consider to be the best ever, it is second-hand, but fairly clean and made secure.

The days in rest I found to be just as hectic as in the forward area, but the feeling of security outweighs all hard work. A great amount of time was spent in arranging men to attend cinemas and clubs, no one ever satisfied with my allotments but that was to be expected.

During the past few days the morale of us all has risen, the news is beginning to look as if Recce should make a dash for it, Americans are pushing south - and our Second Army seems to be making a break through in the Caumont area.

Our S.C.F. had arranged a conference for all the divisional Chaplains, followed by a luncheon at Escotival-Luc-sur-Mer; in view of the supposed shortage, fifteen chaplains had six bottles of 1920 Neuf de Pape, interspersed with Calvados - we were none the worse for such an occasion, a rarity.

On my return we had moved to the middle of a cornfield, but still in Colleville - the air of serenity had passed and we were all standing to, ready to go forward. The Americans had made rapid advances down the Cherbourg peninsular and on 2nd August opposite Caumont opened an attack.

In the evening **2nd August**: we left Colleville and travelled about 25 miles, stopping for the night 10 miles south of Bayeux, the journey was uneventful, but the dust on the roads played havoc with our Carden Lloyds and many broke down, messy dust getting into distributors. We finished digging-in about 2am, my trench was only about 1½ feet, far too hard to dig deeper at such an hour.

Much to my dismay the Rest Room at Colleville had to be closed, the house bore the name of *Jean qui Rit*, named by a Monsieur Favien. Living nearby was a Frenchman who spoke English perfectly, he told me that Austrians occupied the village during the German occupation, and had not their heart in the war, and that on the entry of the 'Tommies', many gave themselves up. He gave me a dramatic description of how they entered the village, and that the sea was described by one of the villagers as being black with the English.

From our harbour near Bayeux we left early in the morning for a small village near Le Bény Bocage, we lived in the grounds of a magnificent château, and the owner when questioned said he was a "gentleman farmer" the only words of English we later learned he knew. We took over the carpenter's shop as an R.A.P., and stayed there the night.

As we came south the countryside changed, there was a wonderful valley running through Le Forêt l'Evêque, it reminded me of the Eshe Valley in Scotland - but the soil was red and reminded of Devon. The people here are easier to understand and they do not have a pronounced accent - at the moment everything is so quiet considering we are so near the German lines, but that I have no doubt will soon all change. The children here have asked me to make them an English 'avion'; this I attempted to do, and as I made it I thought of the day when perhaps I shall make something for Elizabeth.

My personal thoughts centre many and many a time during the day around Margaret and Elizabeth, if only it would end - I am learning no doubt from experience, but experience I fear at a cost.

We attack east of Vire, and 'A' Squadron goes in, the opposition very strong, and ends in forty casualties, the number of killed unknown - we dash forward, I did not arrive until late at night, spent night in a shed, and slept on some hay, a very unsettled night, some shells came over during the morning.

In the the morning I visit the squadrons; they seemed tired. In the evening I buried one man, and on the day following **8/8/44** two more - it was not considered possible to find the other men near the river, for it was under enemy fire.

Those two services were attended by the whole squadron, a divine atmosphere pervaded the service, and a wholehearted sincerity was felt. They brought flowers and made crosses for their comrades; that corner of the field will be for ever England.

I had a visit from the Corps D.A.C.G., very pleasant and most reassuring; his visit made me feel that there is one at least who has not become so absorbed in military affairs that he has lost his spiritual character.

11/8/44. An extremely warm day, feeling somewhat depressed, due to the weather probably, in morning went to front to bury a comrade, he was buried in the corner of a once peaceful orchard - all who stood around were impressed by it all, at the end all standing around cast earth upon the body - each of them in thought and by their actions committed their friend into the hands of God.

Last night I had to arrange the funeral of a French Liaison Officer, he was buried in the churchyard of Gravenie; I had to contact the local curé; not a word of French [2] could he speak, so I laboured somewhat over my mission. The service was not impressive, not a single Latin word could be heard. The Blessing of the Church is all that is needed and there is the only comfort.

On **10/8/4** went to front in armoured car, location west of Vire, upon arrival we saw all men standing to [3], for told Boche had broken through, not healthy - but felt quite cool, and able to presume a coolness, and encouraged one man to get out of his trench and join the rest, I told him that I would stand by him at his post, but of no avail. Impossible to reason with such a case in such surroundings, they must be got away from the line.

11/8/44 Changed location forward over river, and proceeded via Vire, and what a place, houses just shells, the roads had been bulldozed, we arranged a very comfortable R.A.P. in a stable, and looked forward to some good sleep - but away we went further forward, the last stable was worse than the first, whole place [in a] state [of] decay - carcasses lying every-where, smell was awful - at 1.30 we found a cellar but piles of empty and broken bottles to be cleared, there

---

[2] *This is clearly the word used in the Diary, but he probably means 'English'.*
[3] *'Standing to' means being in defensive battle positions, usually because of an imminent threat of attach.*

we slept. Germans had left area in a filthy condition, they leave everything in as an offensive way as they possibly can, excreta and death are all around.

12/8/44 Three cars knocked out on Vire-Tinchebrai Road, two killed, but too near enemy lines to get near them; after three days the M.O. managed to reach them, one was burned beyond recognition, half out of the A.F.V and the other one, Tpr. Opie, our star footballer, crushed on to the wheel - it was most difficult and unpleasant but we extracted their remains - as we undertook this task, the thought of a young life and futility of war impressed itself upon us both - this method is wrong, these lives are needed to build the world. We shall be worse off after this show economically, morally and spiritually.

This has been a week of advancement from Tinchebrai - Flers. Regiment has made its mark - but this advance was at a cost, we lost a number of men, including Peter Gaskell, all very tragic, an awful evening, going backwards and forwards to the A.D.S. I feel thankful that I could be with Peter at the end, and gave him the last rites.

We arrive in Chardun Cordonnière in the early morning after a heavy day, and many a heart-ache for all those who have been mauled and killed - we slept in a stable, but a very disturbed night having been told that snipers lurked in the area. As we lay there footsteps were heard, the officer sat up in bed with his revolver raised, but no one appeared at the door - what could it have been!!!!

The next day we moved on nearer to Flers, crowds of prisoners were coming in - now they say "English goot," how easy to say - but we see their march of devastation.

On Sunday **Aug. 20th** we have a great day, which will always be remembered in the regiment, a Memorial Service was held in8 the field adjoining the Mess. The altar was draped with the Union Jack and the regimental flag flying at half-mast at my back. The C.O. read the roll of honour, which was followed by the words of Binyon.

In the afternoon I visited Miss Sybil Bellairs, who at the outbreak of war was a lecturer in modern languages at Caen University and was placed in a concentration camp, and remained there 2½ years. I have never seen anyone so grateful as she was to see me, and giving her Holy Communion, we had the service in the consulting room of the local doctor: One thing will remain, gratitude and honesty.

The Eight's officers were invited to a Civic Reception of St Paul, our location, and after an oration at the War Memorial, we were invited to a 'Vin d'Honneur,' rather frightening, but most amusing, with very many ancients sitting around, long drooping moustaches, and talking at such speed that it was quite impossible to converse with them in my very halting manner.

We drank white wine and some excellent champagne and they were all very genuine and we were all looked upon as liberators in the true sense.

The feeling of liberation dies away and we all return to our several duties - I conducted the Holy Communion Service with Squadron, and a large parade with 2 Mx.

I paid a visit to D.A.C.G. 8 Corps, a Rev. Wiles, a charming fellow, a Non-Conformist by churchmanship, but very sincere. He provided me the Travelling Church, known as Paul, a picture of St Paul had been painted on the side of the vehicle, with an ascetic smile, not very appropriate.

24/8/44 The Motor Church, S.C.F. and my vehicle proceed in convoy to two of the squadrons, a good crowd came around, a portable harmonium provided the music, and loud speakers were available - the D.A.C.G. gave the men a stirring address - real Baptist fire, they seemed amazed, probably due to my docile sermon which they are more accustomed to.

My morale has gone up considerably, for the Balkan States are giving in; we are all asking amongst ourselves how long can they last out, the first two weeks in September some think, I personally am prepared to bring my date forward from October 31st. We pray that an early ending will not mean Burma - it cannot, I hope, for I must get back to Margaret; she means all to me, around her are centred all my hopes - her letters are an inspiration, I only wish I could have her spirituality.

During the week **24-30 August** a number of Communions were held, and the attendance was reasonable - for a month they averaged about two hundred - this is general in the division.

We still are in a condition of rest, too much of it is apt to lower morale, when men see us advancing towards Germany. During this period a great amount of my time is devoted towards welfare. I do not find that this detracts from the spiritual duties, in fact they have increased in like manner.

3/9/44. We departed from St Paul at mid-day and travelled 150 miles, by-passing Argentan - passing through Bocage - Louviers. On route children threw flowers and fruit into our cars, they all seemed pleased to see us get closer to the retreating Germans - some held up eggs offering them for cigarettes "for Papa." On one occasion during a half hour halt I stopped and turned on my car radio. I soon got an audience, it was rather embarrassing for a very charming mademoiselle presented me with some dahlias in red, white and blue. One could not help being amazed how the women and children are so well dressed, they make themselves look attractive. In spite of four years occupation, their clothes look neat and tidy. It was a wonderful moonlight night, and as we approached the Seine the water glistened and sparkled.

One of the most beautiful sights I have seen was the castle standing on the north bank of the river at Les Andelys, it stood out in grand majesty in moonlight, a fairy tale picture. This castle was built by Richard Coeur de Lion, (why, I have no idea, to me he is associated with the Holy Land, reigned between 1189-1199) castle known as Les Gaillard.

This town the M.O. and I visited the following day, there are two towns adjoining, and both can be seen from the castle. The view from the castle top was magnificent, it possessing a central tower, presumably Richard's command post; beneath it run tunnels. A barbican surrounded the castle itself, and between it and the castle runs a moat. The Germans had used it as a look out.

There are two Churches in the town; both were of the Gothic style, but in one Norman style could be seen, it had been repaired many times and undoubtedly seen many battles.

The bridge opposite the fort had been broken, which we later learned had been blown in 1940 - beside it we had built a Bailey bridge, a proud sight of modern war of thousand of vehicles creeping across nose to tail, of varying tonnage.

Another point worth recording was that in one of the

Churches was hanging a list of rules, relating to Church order and decorum, was 'défense de cracher' - many other rules which would probably have been seen in England during the reign of Charles I. This nation is very backward in its mode of living.

In Les Andelys were two very old buildings, the oldest I have yet seen. Both had a Tudor style - an iron grill covered a glass over the door, on the door posts were two wooden gargoyles, similar to those of the Notre Dame.

Things were all quiet in this area, but from time to time various rumours spread around that Boche are in the woods, but none as yet have been forthcoming. The farms where we are billeted are clean and flourishing - they have found the Germans a profitable proposition, and in some places our reception is looked upon as rather an imposition.

This has been a week of inaction, this period of being away from the line is rather grim, when so much is going on, as we read of advancements and greetings being given on the way. It is hard that this division should be denied what glory there is in war, after it has borne the heat and burden of the day.

Period [of] in-action came to an end, left Saussay de la Campagne on **Sept. 15th**, leaving 6.19 [am], we had a good journey of over 150 miles, some very pleasant country but as we got into Pas de Calais countryside the streets and houses were very dirty. When we reached Beauvais, mist was covering the town, but in the valley it was different, all in patches, with trees showing alone. The battle-fields of 1914-1918 looked desolate and along the route cemeteries were dotted here and there. We stopped near one, and as I walked round I could not help but think of their dying in vain, 26 years from the battle of Somme, their sons were dying. It was at this stop I served the men with tea from my urn, hot sweet tea is always appreciated.

After the halt I took over driving, my driving seat most uncomfortable, one's posterior developed unendurable aches - I drove over the Belgian frontier, and what a grand reception, their flags were draped all along the route, children threw fruit and flowers into our cabin, some children were craving cigarettes for Papa - the route was lined, and finally reached our staging area near Sognies. We messed in the house once owned by the Duke of Aosta, the house had a number of Italian statues, in size it was massive, the front had a colourful array of dahlias and asters; the flowers seemed to flourish in France, every cottage has them in large blooms.

In the evening went into town, and quaffed a glass of Pilsener, it was the best we tasted since 'D' day - we were shaken by the hand by large crowds, some gave us pears and flowers, by the time we reached our car we were a walking fruiterer-cum-florist.

Up again at 3am, feeling very tired, hoping to have reached our area by 1030, but suddenly changed - we by-passed Brussels and Louvain, everyone was most friendly, the houses and gardens were clean, the children looked well cared for: We arrived at Peer, about seven miles from Holland, we messed in the school. The local curé was most helpful, and over a glass of excellent red wine plus cigar we discussed the merits of the High Anglican J.H. Newman, the curé could not understand why authority should hinder one from joining up with Rome.

I slept in a civilian bed, and what a comfortable one, I retired to bed at 9.15 and just passed out, but felt really fit in the morning.

18/9/44 Visited a remarkable house built and designed by a Monsieur Hugo, inside he has made everything from his own design and wonderful sculpturing in cement; one especially of the angel Gabriel bringing the glad news to Blessed Virgin Mary - also a sunflower in the ceiling and in the centre is fixed the electric light. He has etched from the works of Reuben and Rembrandt - everything most artistic, all these things are made to blend and not out of place.

A visit was made to the local Church at Peer, the cleanest and tidiest I have seen since being over here - there was lacking unnecessary ornaments and fewer figures. There is some excellent semi bas-relief above the altars. The ceiling of the nave is brown with coloured cross-pieces, whole place most artistic.

This morning I went to mass; although a Monday there was a large crowd - the whole service was most dignified.

We left Peer at 5.30am and reached quite a pleasant harbour[4], at Vosten Hostie - in the afternoon the M.O. and I went to Escaut Canal to get two bodies from a light recce car - one had his head off, and the other was terribly mangled - the sight was awful, but with ropes around the bodies we managed to drag them through the doors - an 88mm had gone right through the car - the driver managed to escape. Further along the canal bank three civilians were lying dead, having been shot by a German sniper, but as they were lying so close together, probably they had been shot in cold blood.

Our men were buried in the corner of a field, but being below canal level, the water filled a quarter of the grave - during the service a large number of civilians stood around, and a small

---

[4] *A safe overnight assembly area or base away from the battle, usually for tanks or other armoured vehicles.*

girl was carried to place a bunch of flowers on the grave. In the words of one of the troopers "they go in for funerals in these parts."

When I arrived back at the harbour, and not feeling very fit after my unpleasant work - I had to rush off to our A.D.S. - one of our officers had been killed in a motorcycling accident and one officer by enemy action - both having died in hospital - there were others there so I took five that evening.

When I returned the regiment was leaving, just in time - we went over the Canal [Escaut] and have stayed [the] night in a lupin field near Midbuul. On route a large number of Boche were coming in. The Dutch gave us a grand reception and upon arrival at Hamont I stopped and I saw two collaborators being marched off - rumour had it that they were shot - quite probably, for enthusiasm and hate was running high.

In the lupin field 'digging in' was really a pleasure, the soil was soft and we got down four feet in record time and the soil was of a silt nature, and quite comfortable to sleep upon.

We saw a large crowd following a number of collaborators who were being taken to the local gaol, some thought for execution, others considered that they would be put in a concentration camp, they were made to have their hands behind their neck - on the banner was the word 'Traitor'; it was a grim sight, but one must not come to hasty conclusions without knowing the facts, they had betrayed their countrymen.

In another village where one of our squadrons was stationed, an elderly man and woman were caught; the woman's head was shaved and then they were both shot. A better and more humane punishment could be to exclude them from civil rights, denying them the vote and civil appointments.

Girls are dressed in National colours and many of them wear an orange bandeau, either around the head or body.

In the evening of **Sept 21st** many of them danced outside our R.H.Q., music being a piano accordion supplied by one of our troops.

There is a close similarity between many words in our language and Dutch, some are exactly the same, but pronounced with a guttural accent.

The weather during the past few days has been excellent, allowing our spearhead to reach Nijmegen and to-day making headway to Arnhem - this is wonderful news, for they have crossed the Waal, a part of the Rhine, and one at Arnhem is a tributary - now there is no natural obstacle, for both Siegfried and Rhine will be turned. What a tragedy, fortune has turned against us and we have withdrawn from Arnhem, the Germans have fought fiercely to keep this escape route open - nearly two thousand manage to get back [5].

We have advanced slowly, but by the **29/9/44** had reached north of Helmond, our work is mainly guarding a flank.

At a place called Dorplein I had to conduct a funeral of one of my men, it was an impressive service, for the whole population followed the coffin as it was being carried to the grave - there were nuns and priests in the procession, everyone looked upon this man as their village hero, his name will always be remembered there. The body rested for the night in the Seminary and the body was prepared by the nuns for burial the following day.

The people co-operate in a grand way and are most

---

[5] *This is probably intended to mean that the Germans fought fiercely to keep the escape route from Arnhem closed, but nearly 2,000 British 'Paras' managed to escape.*

helpful, they cannot be compared to the French; the French are dirty and their homes are squalid, but with the Dutch all is so different, their kitchens where all the family lives are clean.

We have advanced along the Helmond - Nijmegen axis, everyone gave us an enthusiastic welcome - apples, tomatoes were always at hand to barter for cigarettes. This evening I was told that 30/- would be given for a pound of tea, and one guilder for a cigarette - but a slight exaggeration.

To-day I met a Dutch woman who spoke English fluently, she was a school mistress, and we discussed the Dutch educational system, most extraordinary, but children from the age of twelve are trained for a vocation. Children who are unable to reach a certain standard by the age of fourteen are turned down.

24/9/44 - On Sunday I had to take a funeral near Someren, it was a quiet and eerie journey travelling along a track through a dense wood, an armoured car went in front, and from the Squadron Headquarters I travelled in the armoured car, for snipers were in the area. The village was completely deserted, a very cold night it was, and an extra chill was added by the atmosphere. I returned to regimental headquarters in the pouring rain.

The M.O. and I have been sleeping under canvas, very cold - the last two nights have been living in a house - the good people having given us their parlour.

It is very noticeable in the country how religious minded everyone is, each room has a crucifix, and figures of the Blessed Virgin Mary and St. Joseph. The priest has a real grip upon them all, and churchgoing is a reality. We hear them saying their evening prayers, they intone the Hail Marys: one leads while the others join in the responses.

Today **29/9/44** I took services with 'C' Squadron, a Holy Communion with their H.Q., and short prayers with their troops who were guarding the canal - all these services are most impressive - if only the enthusiasm that is being shown now can be brought back to England, and men's energies centred around their Church what a difference it could make to the Church and Country at large. For the first time many of these men have experienced something of Christ - religion is no longer something ethereal, but a reality, which plays such a great part in the happenings of daily life.

We left Mathysiend on Sunday **Oct. 1st** and travelled to Haps, the owners of our late farm were sorry we left, and came and waved to us frantically. Before we left we were given some eggs, and cigarettes given in return. The people clamour for what they call good cigarettes, a packet of twenty in Holland costs about 40 centimes. When we pass through villages children offer us guilders for chocolate or cigarettes.

On Saturday the M.O. and I visited Helmond, a large and clean town, all the shops were flourishing - we bought some toys for our respective children - mechanical toys can be bought here, whereas in England they are unobtainable. Very ironical for many of them were manufactured in England.

The journey to Haps was uneventful, we got held up on the roads - as we got nearer to the frontier we saw flares being dropped by German planes presumably - we had a comfortable room in a school, quite clean.

On Monday I had to go to Helmond and Bakel to pay billeting money, the latter is always a difficult problem owing to the language question - as I entered I muttered "Burgomeister" to the orderly and was ushered into a palatial room and told by them to pay the money to the Secretary. All this was done in perfect English - my hopes faded, for I [was] sure the secretary [would] never be able to speak English or French - having knocked politely on the door, I entered and the Secretary stood up and said "Good afternoon padre" - most fluent.

The weather has turned very cold, I only hope that winter will not be premature.

Our ten day stay at Haps was very comfortable, we slept in the house of a rose grower, it was most comfortable, and they all were extremely kind, their sitting room was always open to us, and we were given coffee and lots of fruit. We slept in a small room upstairs, the M.O. had a magnificent bed, and I my camp bed in the corner.

One very interesting day was spent in an O.P. at St. Agatha's monastery, it was situated about 300 yards from the River Meuse, we could see German territory, and Germans moving about, it was quite a thrill to be so near and see them without being observed yourself. Very few locals were living there, and there was only a skeleton staff in residence, they were of the Dominican Order. They each had small rooms, not too spartan, at this moment I could call them palatial. They had some magnificent oil paintings hanging on the walls, many old masters, but it was too dark to see them properly. I tried to get down again to see them, but shells came down in large numbers which prevented me. There was a large field which was under observation by the enemy, which always needed strategy to cross.

Mentioning O.P.s, I went to the top of a windmill at Beffelt, but the visibility was poor, we saw Germans moving about from place to place very quickly - we saw our shells bursting on a brick factory with precision.

Many of these villages are visited by the Boche each evening, they cross the river at night by boat, one night they penetrated our troop position, and got shot up.

While at Haps the S.C.F. wanted me to go to Brussels with him for one night which in the end turned out to be two and three days, not very satisfactory. We stayed at St. George's Chaplain Club, which was very comfortable, it was once a Senior German Officers' Club, they left behind them 3,000 bottles of wine, but before we arrived they had been looted by the Belgians, but loot is the wrong word perhaps: I saw the play *Arms and the Man* by G.B.S[6]., which took one's mind away from the war, it reminded me of the good old days, when M. and I were together. While at the Club I met D.C.G. Hughes; he is an excellent fellow, not of the regular stamp, it is quite refreshing to meet a high ranking Chaplain not of the same mentality as so many regulars.

The attack on Overloon began on **Oct. 14th,** progress was extremely slow, in spite of a tremendous barrage which went on throughout all Sunday and Monday, the Germans have been fighting stubbornly - on the 16th eleven deserters came into our lines, most amazing, and one of them an SS. If this feeling of frustration exists amongst them, it must equally apply to many others - the question is why do they not pack it in?

17/10/44 Patrols of the East Yorks in Venray, by the

[6] *George Bernard Shaw.*

evening it may have fallen, the news looks better to-night, for the Yorks are coming in from the West, it may soon be outflanked.

This morning I went out to one of our Squadrons, but found myself on the main Venray road, only two miles from the town. I made a hasty retreat, having taken the wrong turning. When I got to the correct road I checked in, and met the C.O., never to live down my bad map reading.

This afternoon I have been around with a Dutch liaison officer, a very useful person to have when paying billeting money and obtaining eggs etc. He is a Protestant, and told me that in this part of Holland, the people have very large families, and it is not uncommon to see families of twenty and twenty-five - what a thought. The priest has a great hold over his people, and to go against him is a sin.

17/10/44 - An awful night, rain swept the open country, we got very wet in going to the Mess - the artificial moonlight gave the place an eerie feeling - this light is made by searchlight and helps drivers in supplying the forward troops, and those out on patrol:

18/10/44 - My temper this morning is at a high pitch, for the welfare wireless set has been stolen from the house, civilians who once occupied the building are considered to be the thieves, to-morrow the interpreter will get to work. Other sets were due to arrive to-day from 'B' Squadron, but as yet no sign of them.

I have made a number of visits to the forward areas during the past few days, the feeling in the stomach which once existed very acutely in France is now only half as bad, not because the risk is less, it may be I am getting used to the atmosphere, but this can never be. Mines are now a greater menace, and great care has to be taken. I have instructed my driver to have sand-bags filled and to be put into the driving cab, these sand-bags are most uncomfortable when driving, but better I would rather have cramp in legs and posterior, than be blown twenty feet into the air.

23/10/44 - We are still on the outskirts of Oploo, but the weather has improved, and our billet has greatly improved, the windows have been mended by our skilful Sgt. Harbottle, the doors have been blocked up, and all is well - rain will always find the crevices, but other measures are employed when that enemy breaks through.

For the past four days I have had to conduct a funeral, one man killed by interfering with a probable booby-trapped bazooka. To-day I had to help in extricating a Sgt, whose car had been hit by a bazooka, he was in a terrible mess, and it was so difficult to get him clear, blood was splashed everywhere inside, the two survivors got the vehicle back to the harbour. Sgt. Dodds was a cheerful soul, and always had a kind word to say to all. Two of us managed to get him out and wrapped him in a blanket. These last few days life has been very hectic in contacting all my units.

Yesterday I had perhaps one of the most impressive evening services I have ever held, this one was held in a barn with straw on either side, the men fixed an electric light in one corner, and from the candles on the altar we all worshipped God - God was there and refreshed we went away.

These services have their humorous sides, and one with

the R.E's was held in a cow shed, calves occasionally disturbed the service, but a cat found its way in through the congregation, and immediately began to make a hole and carry out a law of nature - was its journey really necessary - presumably so.

As I sit here with a candle as my light, I must look like Adam Bede less the quill pen. Margaret and Elizabeth are before me, how I long for all this to come to an end, they seem so far away, and even now one cannot but help feeling homesick - why should all this fall upon our generation - there is always the feeling of insecurity, that one may not get back to ones we love so much, this comes over me when near the enemy, when things of all calibres are falling around; but it all goes and back man goes about his business.

24/10/44 - This has been a hard day, starting at 0830 for the cemetery and arranged for grave to be dug - I visited Corps H.Q. at Handel, and one of my squadrons - I went to an R.A.M.C. Field Ambulance H.Q., and made enquiries about services, they hadn't had one for a long time, someone is not doing their work. They have been invited to a H.C. of mine with 'A' Squadron. I must take them under my wing - my units increase daily.

In the afternoon I had to conduct three funerals, their bodies had been retrieved from the minefield, one man was in small pieces, and when wrapped in a blanket, one man could carry it - the means of identification of such cases is so difficult, and can only be marked as unknown. The Bde. Cemetery at Oploo is beginning to grow, small white crosses are placed in line, and civilians place small bunches of flowers, and tend to the graves.

I was impressed by the R.E. officer who helped me with the bodies, the one who was in pieces he wanted to carry himself and place in the grave, he said "He is one of my men and I want to carry him, padre" - such humaneness exists amongst all these men, they are in the midst of death throughout the day in lifting mines. All this softens any man - we are no longer hard creatures, and find it so hard to control our emotions when one of ours is laid to rest.

The stay at the monastery has been extremely comfortable, we had a palatial bedroom with central heating, and I slept on a bed which when not in use folded against the wall. I was most fortunate in being able to have my services in the refectory, there was always a good attendance, and the services went well with the help of a grand piano, a musical instrument always makes a service, one is able to attempt new hymns, and lead the men with tunes they do not know.

The priests are of a teaching order and I find them most helpful in every kind of way:

Nearby to the monastery of St. Josef is a nunnery, the nuns kindly washed my laundry and I do not think I have ever found such kindliness and gentleness as exists here - they work in the fields during the day, and their life must be arduous.

Even at the monastery we were not away from the shells, for nearly every morning the Boche would send over about eight 105mm shells, but by good luck they fell around the building - but lying in bed and hearing the sound coming nearer was always very disturbing not knowing if it would hit the building:

A squadron generally came out of the line after a week and spends four days in rest - this gives me the opportunity to see them and help with any welfare problems.

I formed a Rest Room in the monastery and it was well patronised, I put my car radio there, but as usual someone would interfere with it and it would fail to work. I have come to the conclusion that the majority of troopers are irresponsible, and do not value anyone's property - they throw the papers on the floor, and take anything that does not belong to them. But nevertheless this room has served a useful purpose, and it has been appreciated by the majority:

We now find ourselves below Overloon and Venray, a most depressing place with not a single house whole, the one storey building we are in has its roof off, but two of the rooms are comparatively dry, and in one of them we sleep - the remainder sleep in the cellar.

We have developed the technique now of getting into a place, and in spite of how bad it may be we can always make it comfortable in a short time - a light, table and photographs on the table make the surroundings homely; it has been raining now for two days and the roads are indescribable, and vehicles are easily bogged as soon as they go off the road. During the past month there have been very few casualties - one yesterday, a man being blown up on a mine.

I find now that we must get more mine conscious, as the Germans are placing them indiscriminately as they retreat - this is one thing I have developed, namely being mine conscious, a good trait.

Today **23/11/44** waiting to move has been most tiring, and this evening I have rather a headache, the weather is the cause of all this.

From October - January we have found ourselves

opposite the Meuse, on the whole it is quite peaceful, but the whole area has been terribly battered, it is difficult to find any accommodation that is in one piece.

There is very little to write these days, not because things are not happening, but because the news is of a routine nature, and not of interest to anyone.

2/2/45 - I am now acting S.C.F., living in a medico's house in Deurne, Holland. This house is extremely comfortable, my bedroom adjoins my office on the first floor, there are armchairs, a wireless and telephone which goes to make a room civilised. For the first time since coming over here I have used a typewriter. This job is certainly not difficult or arduous, and anyone with a slight idea of administration can hold it down. There is one drawback, that I am tied and unable to get round my men as often as I would like, but I guess I shall soon return to the monastery and become normal again.

3/2/45 - Just now things are much in the air, the feeling of expectation seems to be on the lips of us all and the German[7] offensive fifty miles from Berlin has certainly altered things on this front, and any moment now we may begin to advance into the Reich.

The weather since Christmas is worth recording, it has at times been bitterly cold, and a great deal of snow and ice covered the ground - but within the past few days the thaw has set in, and the roads are beginning to break up, it is amazing to see what can happen to roads, and the ones which were once reasonably good roads for travelling are now more like tracks. Large gangs of R.E's are working on them, and a number of

---

[7] *Probably intended to say Russian, not German.*

collaborators are supposed to be taking part in road repair - a great deal of the time they spend leaning on their shovels. Those who are not collaborators do not seem to be wholehearted in making the war machine run smoothly - I sometimes think that they are nearly all tempered with a German sympathetic outlook, but that of course may be just my own personal ideas, but we are very near to the frontier.

Life in the Maas progressed very satisfactorily, life was full of routine duties, service were taken over a very wide area.

There was a heavy fall of snow during January and February and the roads were made impassable in many places. But worse was to follow, for during the thaw the roads completely broke up, roads which were reasonable, within two days became like ploughed fields, vehicles became bogged. At Stevensbeck the whole regiment less two squadrons was isolated, and they had to make a road over the fields with fir trees.

We moved about **Feb. 8th** to Lubbeck near Louvain, Belgium, there we really enjoyed ourselves and it was most comfortable. I was living with the M.O. in the gardener's cottage, and the men were billeted in private houses. This helped the men's morale, and they all enjoyed themselves, and soon became one of the family, they are our best ambassadors. The men were able to go to Brussels and Louvain.

On **23rd Feb**. we heard we were to move, undoubtedly to support the attack which had already gone in near Emmerich, the Canadians and the 15 Scottish had got through the Reichwald, but were meeting some very stiff opposition.

My leave was due on the **26th Feb.**, but a terrible wave of duty first impelled me to tell the C.O. that I was prepared to stay and go with the unit but he was definite that I should go for there was always the possibility that the unit might not be deployed. On Saturday morning I went by car to Brussels and stayed there until Monday, it was most boring, as I did not know anyone. I went to the Symphony at the Beaux d'Arts, it was most delightful - I thoroughly enjoyed Dvorak's *New World*, and Beethoven's 5th - the cello solo by Lalo left me completely cold, just a conglomeration of discords, but just my bad taste I guess, for the audience rose and applauded. The audience are more enthusiastic than the English.

I left Brussels at 9pm on Monday **26th Feb.**, everything had been arranged in a wonderful way, with not a single hitch, we were given tea and buns at Lille, and arrived at Calais about 7.30 am; there our passes were stamped, given breakfast and money changed. We embarked at about 1.15pm and arrived Dover at 4.30, the weather was fine and the journey from Dover to London was perfect.

As we got nearer to London my excitement grew more intense - having made my own way down the platform, of course leading the way, I got a taxi after some difficulty, but soon reached Claridges, there to meet Margaret - it was all too wonderful, words are inadequate to put it all down in black and white. There was so much to say, which could not be written, one of the most thrilling moments in my life.

We had the most blissful and wonderful seven days, which went all too quickly - seeing the Aunts was another thrill - to think they are so comfortable, they so long for my return.

Those seven days were just like a dream, how I long for the day when there are to be no more partings.

That drive to Watford was very grim, and how I hated it, but we consoled ourselves with the thought that the next leave would be the end of all.

Victoria station was a most strange sight; thousands of men, some of them very drunk, shouting and singing, drowning their sorrows, that I presume is one way. But I found my friends there quite cheerful which did my morale good, we shared our ideas etc., and so went on our way rejoicing. We left Victoria at 11.30 for Dover and there transported to Duke of Connaughts barracks, what a barn of a place it was, I had a small bed and my mattress was a palliasse, my feet protruded over the end, an awful night's sleep, that of course was to be expected.

In the morning an amazing sight was witnessed at the breakfast table, very glum faces, some very cantankerous, demanding this and that. We whiled away the hours playing shove-ha'penny, and the remainder of the time was spent in eating and getting money changed.

The Channel crossing was uneventful, I slept in my cabin, upon arrival we walked about a half mile to a train which only went about five miles, and we were detrained and spent some hours in a barrack of a place, had tea and supper, and then entrained for our final journey. We slept and talked, ate one another's rations - my small bottle of brandy was greeted in a hilarious manner, this was split amongst four of us.

23rd March: The past few days have been really heavenly, and to-day even better and we are now on the eve of great events for the B.L.A. Zero hour is drawing near. This afternoon we were briefed for the forthcoming operation, although we ourselves are not in the active assault we have been given a fair idea of our future role, which should be extremely interesting. I am writing this in the open-air, beneath a bank in the Siegfried defences; pine trees surround me, it is a grand place to come and think; a magnificent blue hue comes up as the sun begins to set, which adds to the beauty; the birds are singing and a brown squirrel occasionally scampers by, and climbs the tallest tree, he peers cheekily round a branch, the first time he has seen khaki maybe.

The Germans have gone to a great deal of trouble in erecting defences, never to be used. The rusty barbed wire rather spoils the beautiful wood - occasionally one comes across an ammunition dump, everything scattered about, there I walk warily for fear that they may have booby trapped the dump, or laid the odd mine. This is a wonderful evening, planes keep constantly droning overhead, in the distance there is a crump. To-day I have read some of those delightful short poems of A.E. Housman. Some of them are rather morbid, but very stirring.

This is a very exciting evening, and we shall all wait patiently for the opening of the barrage - I hope we may see the airborne going in - this operation cannot be a failure, the whole thing is based as a 'D' day operation. The war cannot last long, he is losing thousands of men a day. Patton has taken over 100,000 in the Moselle region. But I will not be too optimistic, for I know I was a false prophet far back in the Normandy days. The day for the Rhine crossing is nearing its climax; on Friday and Saturday the roads became clogged and my wings became clipped; this was an awful bore, but my time is well occupied in dealing with various welfare problems.

I was told to-day **26/3/45** that I had received the 'C in C' certificate, this did not elate me tremendously, for I have only done my job. The presentation was made in Army Orders and Regt. Orders, with the C.O.'s congratulations.

On **26/27th Mar.** we crossed the Rhine, a tremendous bombardment took place on Wesel and the S.S. Bde[8] assaulted the town with slight casualties, a further crossing was made by 51, 53, and 15 Divs: each of them made a satisfactory bridgehead. Throughout the whole day the sky was dotted with planes. At the time of the crossing we were kept back at Welbeck near Army HQ. On Monday evening we were given four hours notice to move, and left at 0900 hrs: we went through the [6th] Guards Bde, our intention was to cross the river and stay the night outside Wesel. There was a constant stream of traffic, the Americans were blocking the roads and as usual travelling at top speed, the amount of equipment they possess is enormous.

The journey to the Rhine was packed with a number of incidents; for instance Gelden near Welbeck was still burning, houses just gutted; these presented an eerie spectacle in the bright moonlight. The Luftwaffe put in far too many appearances for my liking, on one occasion when standing by my truck watching tracer bullets soaring into the sky, a real Brock display, a Dornier 210 I heard coming zooming down between the trees, my driver and I flung ourselves to the ground. As he came over I could see the crosses, he used cannon shell which exploded all around me, our Medical Sergeant was hit in the arm, there was another slight casualty - real luck for us all: as one got near

[8] *Special Service Brigade - commandos.*

the river planes zoomed around, but did not drop any bombs.

The Rhine crossing was a real feat of engineering, it was an American pontoon, steel girders placed on top of rubber boats, a very strong current was running, it was remarkable to think that a great part of the American Army and part of the British had crossed at the point.

We are from now onwards under command of 6th Gds. Armd. Bde. We arrived at our harbour south of Wesel. I slept with the MO in a sitting-room which was quite comfortable, but we could only get about 2½ hours. We stayed there most of the day, I was left i/c of Rear HQ, which is an awful bore, for I so wanted to get up with Tac. HQ[9]. Late evening I went to Schermbeck or rather on the outskirts, we slept in a field in a tent, quite a good night, one had to dig a trench because occasional shells kept coming over. In the morning we moved further, and after a certain amount of persuasion I managed to go with Tac., much more exciting and I was able to be kept in the picture. The amount of armour moving forward was a most impressive sight, Churchills with American infantry sitting on the tanks and prisoners were coming back but very slowly.

In the afternoon we moved forward and passed through Dorsten, a large town on the north part of the Rhine, not a [large] number of industries - the town was badly damaged with shelling and and bombing, as we entered the Germans in the nearby woods were sending over air-bursts, we passed through the town and stayed a few hours north of it. Here there was much activity dealing with German wounded, one of them I helped to carry across a ploughed field to a German aid-post, what a weight he was by the time we got to the end of our journey. At this point machine gun fire was coming from the

---

[9] *Tactical Headquarters the forward HQ in the Battle area.*

wood by the road, a most unpleasant cross-roads with a German 88 firing only a few hundred yards away, but all went well. I arrived back at our harbour just in time to go with the column to Lippramsdorf which is near Haltern, the roads were littered with German transport, a German 88mm had been by-passed en route, it was well camouflaged and undoubtedly was the gun which caused so much trouble at the crossroads. Houses were burning at every point along the route, the smell of death and burning was awful.

We reached our harbour in a very boggy field, it was raining and being dark also did not help matters. Our first job was to dig in as shells were falling perilously near. We could only dig about 3½ feet for water began to well up into the trench. We thought that we should be staying the night so we dug our trench to accommodate the M.O. and myself. We got our tent erected over the trench, by now one had had very little sleep, and I began to feel extremely tired. After some supper casualties came in, one man had been killed, a Sgt Rasworthy, he will be a great loss as he was one of my most ardent communicants, always willing to help. I buried him in the darkness at about mid-night. As I stood there over the trench with two sergeants from R.H.Q. I felt an amazing feeling of the Divine presence, across the road an ammunition dump was going up, tracer bullets soaring into the air, shells exploding, but yet Christ was near for that short time. By noon I was feeling really dog'O, but the M.O. called me into the tent and said a wounded man wanted to speak to me. I went into the tent and knelt by the stretcher, and holding his hand we said a silent prayer. He also was one of my ardent supporters, when he came round sufficiently he promised me that he would write me a letter in hospital.

At 12.45 I retired to my hole, and immediately went off to sleep, but I was awakened at 1.15 by a whistle and told to move in a half hour's time. Dressed quickly and dismantled everything and ready for the road again. We were to enter the outskirts of Haltern about eight miles further on. By some bad luck we got detached from the main column which flashed on without ensuring that others were coming up in the rear. There were only three vehicles, ambulance, jeep and light recce. car, and not being too sure of the route was also adding to our confusion, for the Boche were on either side of the road. The whole road was deserted, and anything might have happened, eventually we caught up with the remainder of the regiment, but that drive was a most unpleasant 15 minutes.

We reached the outskirts of Haltern about 3am. There was a certain amount of uncertainty about the place being really cleared. We stopped opposite a cafe which we broke into, I slept on a sofa, but it was a very disturbed night.

In the morning work began in full force, wounded Germans poured in, and prisoners were coming by in long columns, looking most dejected. Our casualties since crossing the Rhine had been fairly light, one very remarkable incident was that a Sgt. who opened the door of his light recce car and an armoured piercing shell went through the door and out the other side: In Haltern we had our mess in the town adjoining a mill, our room was somewhat chaotic as I had to share it with other officers.

This time we left early in the morning, but before going to our location I had to get two men out of an armoured car who had been burned to death. It was another of those unpleasant sights which I had to witness in France; they were so badly charred that the smell was not so unpleasant as I had previously imagined.

On the way to the Squadron we picked up three prisoners who came out of the wood holding a white flag tied to a stick. A very good thing they did not become aggressive for we should have become easily overwhelmed.

Our next area was outside Dulmen, and what a mess the place was in, we had bombed it well and truly, and not a house was standing. We spent a whole day in this field which was most dull, my dullness was broken with visits to the Squadrons. I went with the C.O. in his Dingo[10], which was very near to the line, or more truly where the Germans were, for there is no fixed line here, which makes it occasionally very difficult for one never knows when you will be fired upon.

That particular afternoon I went to a squadron and saw the [6th] Guards Tank Bde in action, the first time that I have seen a tank fire in anger, they were firing at a Tiger Tank which had been hidden in the wood a few hundred yards away. The Germans retaliated with mortar, which was the signal to take cover.

That night I spent in an awful house, the ceiling had caved in, and rain came through, but with a certain amount of manipulation with my bed, I slept well, and nothing disturbed me.

The next day the **31st March** we made a steady advance towards Münster, we went from one harbour to another, and finally ended up north-east of Nottuln, the journey took us through some beautiful woods, and we bivouacked for the night in a hay-field, it

---

[10] *A small, wheeled, armoured reconnaissance vehicle.*

was raining hard at the time, and we got very wet and somewhat depressed waiting for Rear HQ to arrive with my tent and necessary kit. After some difficulty we erected our tents and bedded down at 1 am.

It had been a tiring day with very little work to do. I always find that in battle, little I can do, except raising the morale of the sick and wounded. The next day we moved on again, having left this awful field near Roxel early in the morning.

It was **April 1st**, Easter Sunday, what a wonderful way to spend in killing or being killed. The M.O. and I left after the main column, and by misfortune we took the wrong turn and found ourselves on the outskirts of Roxel which had not been taken, as soon as we stopped and consulted our map, a Spandau[11] opened up, into our vehicle we jumped, and drove off at top speed, we were emulating Brooklands in our take off, the rear light nearly hit the headlamps.

We made for Nienberge under caution, the town was being shelled by an 88mm and flak guns when we arrived, but there were no casualties - we lived in the house of a high Nazi official who had fled with the Germans. The caretaker was made to hand over his firearms, and from the collection I got an excellent 16 bore, and a large quantity of cartridges. The house had a typical Nazi air, portraits of 'The Bête Noir', Swastikas etc. They had an excellent supply of eggs upon which we fared sumptuously, after half an hour upon arrival I had two of them fried.

Throughout the day I could not but help thinking that it was Easter Sunday; it made me feel so depressed, the first time that I had missed a service on that day. I went round the troops

---

[11] *A German medium, machine gun.*

who were in the line and just reminded them of the day, they all reminisced about the good old days, what Church they used to attend etc.

Our mess in this house was quite pleasant, purple tulips were on the dining room table, and a few bottles of wine in the cellar, which were consumed at dinner. We slept in a very dirty room at the back of the house, much filth had to be swept up before we could get down to a good sleep.

On Monday **April 2nd** we were still in Nienberge, and our Sqn. Comd., Major Rayer was badly wounded in the leg, it was most unfortunate. I went to see him, but it was most unpleasant for light flak guns and two 88 mms overlooked our position: I went to our forward O.P. and saw the guns through my glasses; they were well camouflaged, but far too near for my liking - we had to run across an open stretch of country, the 100 yards was done in good time.

We left Nienberge on Tuesday morning and went to a very delightful farm near Greven - N.E. of Münster, it was all very comfortable, and in those two days I was able to have Easter Services with my Sqns and write a number of letters, not forgetting the personal maintenance, in my house there was a bath, but no hot water this had to be boiled, but then much dirt was shed.

After two days we left the Gds. Armd. and 16th American Airborne to join 3rd Br. Inf. Div.[12] - we had a long and tedious journey, and went into Holland near Enschede. This town is just over the border, they had only been liberated four days, and what a contrast, flags greeted us, cheering children by the roadside. This reminded me of our September days, we were

---

[12] *3rd British Infantry Division.*

billeted in a most comfortable house, mattresses, bathroom etc, but as usual this was only short lived and we left at 11.30, travelling through Nordhorn to Gordhuoe, here we came into the battle again, guns were firing, and artificial light lit up the whole sky. I did not get into the harbour until about 4.30 am, reason for the lateness, that I got split off from the main column, and went into the front area, when I got past the guns and hearing other front line noises, I decided to retrace my path.

We did not stay long in this very unpleasant area, but I managed to find a place to sleep for about three hours, in a dirty room, but when I awoke the sun was shining and it was a beautiful day. Why I was energetic at that hour amazes me, for I called the officers with tea, and made myself extremely unpleasant with early morning cheerfulness.

From this harbour we went quite a short distance to a German cavalry barracks at Lingen and one of the largest cavalry barracks I have yet seen; there must have been accommodation for nearly three hundred horses, an indoor riding school, and spacious grounds for training. This barracks had been held by German N.C.O.'s, but were overcome by the divisional infantry. Rear and Main Div. were also in the barracks, and I had an opportunity to hear some of the latest scandals - much to be told having been away from the Div. for so long. The D.A.A.G., Ven. Lloyd asked me if I could help him to write a citation for the C.O. regarding a D.S.O. I did not realise how difficult this was, for actual facts have to be given, and as far as I can see only the person who gives the orders is able to supply the necessary answers. In the afternoon I had a sleep in my tent, and managed to catch up with what had been lost the previous night.

That evening about ten o'clock some Army Radar troopers' billet caught fire, and one man was burned to death, they had lit a large fire in their bedroom about 12' x 6' and had a full petrol can in the room which had exploded. By the time I got to this scene things were in a state of chaos, volumes of smoke pouring out of the building, but the fire was soon got under control. By the time we had finished clearing up, it was nearly 1 am. The next day I buried the man consumed in the fire, and in the afternoon we left for a small village near Estringen [possibly not the correct name]. It was a lovely day, and I was anxious to get round visiting my units, but it was impossible as they were all on the move again; I saw my F.D.S. for a few minutes.

We slept in a very comfortable house, and I managed to find a mattress, but our sleep was to be very short, for we had reveille at 4am and from then on an immediate notice to move, but time went by, the notice was constantly being postponed, and eventually we did not leave until about midnight. I have never felt so bored, just lounging around and waiting. The reason for the delay was that a bridge had collapsed over which the main divisional traffic had to pass.

My time was not completely wasted for I found some dead Boche who had been killed beside their flak guns; they were buried beside their guns.

I cannot understand why they keep on fighting, for the Americans have got up to the Elbe on a hundred mile front, and have crossed the river in force - they now are only 20 miles from the Czech frontier, and the Russians have captured Vienna - the Ruhr pocket is steadily collapsing, and virtually the country has been split in two.

We then began our all night move to near Bremen; it was an excellent night and we were allowed to use whatever lights we required. My driver drove from 12-2.30, and I from then till 7; we passed through Rheine and by-passed Osnabrück, it was very lonely [or lovely?] country and the keep-awake tablets kept us both alert. We reached our small village, which was quite pleasant, and being a delightful warm day, I got down to some personal maintenance and washing, it certainly was a relief - we stayed in Levern for one night, but had to be ready to move by 0900 hrs.

We were ordered to move in blocks as enemy aircraft were becoming more active and had been strafing our convoys, again a lovely day, and an enjoyable run, on the way we passed hundreds of slave workers who had been released from their camps; they were all hiking back in a real joyous mood. Russians with S.U.[13] painted on their backs dressed in a green uniform, French in khaki - in fact there was nothing uniform about them, just a motley crowd - they had taken their taskmasters' best horse and cart, and anything that moved from car to bicycle, they marched and saluted in their way to each vehicle that moved forward.

We arrived at a delightful village called Heiligenloh, and we had the best officers mess ever, comfortable chairs, and pleasant beds, the owner had a distillery, and he was ordered to hand over large quantities of gin, this he did willingly - these people appear to be cooperative, but still we must remember that they are Nazi at heart. There was a small lake in the garden on which we rowed; it would be grand if we could go back there for the occupation, but I fear no such luck.

While there I had some services with the squadron which

---

13 *Possibly 'Sowjetisch Unmenschlich' - Soviet Subhuman.*

were well attended. I managed to get around to my units, but great care has to be taken in travelling for certain roads are blocked with small enemy pockets. We stayed here for three nights and left for an open field near Twistingen and Bassum, the regiment was not heavily employed and in the evening I walked through the woods with my gun and shot a rabbit and pigeon, there are some woods nearby which have deer in them, but rumour has it that there are Boche also.

This is a very delightful field, and here we spent two nights, my shooting only produced one rabbit and a pigeon. One afternoon I spent in writing and getting up-to-date with a number of welfare problems, they are most difficult when in the field, and the men are not always available.

It was here that Margaret told me that my name was being considered for the job of Youth Organiser in the St. Albans diocese. The very thought of it thrills me, if only this war would end, so that I could get on with a real job. A padre in the Forces is greatly hampered by rules and regulations, and as we are constantly on the move, day after day it is well nigh impossible to travel to one's outside units and give them services. In order to arrange a service one has to pay two visits, and also to make quite certain that they have not moved overnight.

17/4/45 - We are having a number of casualties as a result of mines, the Germans in this sector are desperately trying to delay our advance, but we are making very slow progress. 3rd Div. seems to have lost some of its old drive, it is certainly not considered the first class division as when in the Normandy bridgehead. There are many reasons, but I am not fully in the picture. I am not in a position to judge.

To-day Bill Purkiss of 'A' Sqn was slightly wounded as a result of a shell, and was returning to harbour sitting on a L.R.C. when it backed into a gateway and went over a mine, both his legs were blown off. I have been to the 84th General [Hospital] to see him, and there is every possibility of him surviving, but he has had his legs amputated, it is very sad, as he was an excellent cricketer. Great care has to be taken in travelling, because a vehicle has been there before you, it does not mean that all is well, for generally it is only by constant pressure and by vehicles running over the earth that they explode, for the mines have been dug deep into the earth.

From our pleasant field we moved to Klosterseelte, not such a pleasant harbour; we had to move at night, over frightful tracks, and only by good luck did we manage to get there for the tracks had very deep ruts - my 15 cwt. stands up to the wear and tear in a grand style - but now my driver is away on leave, it is very tiring reading a map and driving. We only stayed there about 18 hours, and moved a few miles further forward to Kirchseelte.

17/4/45 was a lovely day, and I had to travel from one sector to another to take funerals and services. As I was returning in the evening, we had a storm, and it rained torrentially and hailed; I had to stop my car, for I could only see a few yards in front of me, the hail stones were as large as pigeon's eggs, the largest I have ever seen. Our tent is pitched in a small orchard, with a beautiful cherry tree in full bloom.

My activities to-day **18/4/45** have been hampered by a threat of a further move which is most annoying. But I have dealt with varied welfare problems - only hope now that we shall not move during the night, which to my mind is unnecessary.

A few days ago in Baustrift I met a German pastor, who had been imprisoned for denouncing Goebbels from his pulpit; they were most charming, and told me their story, how the Gestapo in Münster where he lived simply controlled the town, their two sons had been press-ganged into the Army, but both were now prisoners of war. Their only fear now was the slave workers who had been released from their cages, but I personally do not think they need worry, as their one ambition is to get back to their country as quickly as they possibly can. There have been only isolated incidents of an outbreak of violence - that sometimes has been warranted, for their taskmasters must have been most unkind to them.

From **17th - 21st April** we spent at Kirchseelte which was very pleasant, we have a cherry tree overhanging our tent, the field is very damp and when we left the M.O.'s truck got bogged, but I managed to get out and summon to his aid an armoured car.

As I was going up to Gt. Machenstadt, our new harbour I saw our signal truck go up on a mine, no-one was hurt but the vehicle just disintegrated; a tank which it was passing at the time also hit a mine and had its tracks blown off. It has been thought that the civilians living nearby had laid them, but it was only conjecture, and with no proof to work on.

We had a pleasant house while here; I got round to see some of my units which were at Brinkum near Bremen preparing for the attack; my services were very well attended. While here

I had an excellent view of the bombing of Bremen.

From the **Apr. 23rd -26th** Mitchells and Lancasters came over and bombed the place incessantly, huge columns of smoke came up in great billows as each bomb went down.

I went to a forward O.P. on the night of the attack, and everything opened up, tracer and shells by the thousand were poured into the town, the whole place was an inferno in a short time. In the morning I saw our Typhoons gunning the moving German columns leaving the town; in that town two things were standing, the cathedral with its twin spires and the city hall. It was extremely interesting sitting in the attic of our house, which has the O.P., seeing our shells come over and falling only about five hundred yards ahead on the German positions - needless to say there was no retaliation, in good Geordie language they "kept their heads down."

The following day I went into part of the town; it was still burning, refugees were coming back, things began to smell, from cattle, dead on the roadside, and civilians who had been killed in the buildings.

The Sappers had done a grand job in this battle, and my old 17th[14] are first class, real thugs but men who will lift any kind of mine, from sea mines to booby traps. The other day I went and saw them, still as cheerful as ever, always a smile and a shout of encouragement. They always have tea on the brew, and generally before one has time to get out of the car, a mug of tea is thrust into your hand, generally with the dirt of months caked around the sides, but I drink it, for to do otherwise would offend them terribly.

The war seems to be coming to a close, but we still are

[14] *17th Regiment Royal Engineers.*

having casualties; at the moment we are not doing any real recce. work, but holding and expanding a flank. The Boche in this Delmenhorst sector are laying sea mines, and the other day two were laid in the verges and when our carriers went by them they exploded killing twelve men. These men were in the R.U.R's[15]. Great care has to be taken not to go on the verges, for any moment you might go up in smoke, one consolation being sudden death sudden glory - but not for me - a more congenial passing, I hope.

We moved on the **30th Apr.**, to Delmenhorst, into the headquarters of the National Socialist Party; it was a very quiet week for the regiment with only one squadron in action. I used to go up regularly to them, they had two men killed from mines which is so sad with the war coming to an end.

This week is full of events - Italian campaign coming to an end so suddenly, and the capitulation of over 100,000 men.

On the morning of **4th May** cease fire came to the armies in N.W. Europe which meant that for us war had finished.

It is impossible to record in any detail one's reactions to all this - there are two words which are in the forefront of my mind; one is thankfulness, and the other a sense of security. No longer will the odd shell come out of the blue and do its worst. I saw some men in the afternoon prior to the cease fire, they all realised that the end was near, and for the first time did I hear them express their feelings about going out on patrol, they considered the risk far too much at that stage. They had not to go on patrol, so their fears were allayed.

We stayed at Delmenhorst for over a week; it was a

[15] *Royal Ulster Rifles.*

pleasant town, the most amazing thing was to see the German policemen conducting traffic in their military uniforms, when we first entered the town, we wondered at first if we had misread our maps.

Any moment now Victory Day might dawn upon us, in case I should not have things under control I prepared the form of service and began my address.

On **May 4th** we moved to a small village called Schieldhern; it is delightfully situated in a small valley about eight miles from Osnabrück, the Officers Mess stands on the east slope and overlooks the opposite side, with beautiful green trees, and undulating country. This undoubtedly is a holiday resort in peace time by the number of hotels in the area. One of these hotels we have taken over as a club for the men which is to be called 'St. George and the Dragon', we hope to give the men snacks and beer. I also have a small chapel which is being called 'The Chapel of St. George'.

At the moment I am using the Lutheran Church, which to my amazement has a Catholic touch about it, there is a crucifix on the Altar and four large candles. The Bible is placed in the centre, and the font in the sanctuary. There is no prayer desk. How glad one is to get to a place with an atmosphere and away from those awful hovels where so much improvisation has to be done in order to make it look like or resemble any place of worship.

The men are coming well to the services, and on **Victory Day May 8th** we had a quarter of an hour service which was extremely well attended. I do hope and pray that the standard and response which was reached while in battle will remain now. Everything points to things going well.

It is now three weeks since we began occupational duties and on the whole things have fared well. But a curious change has come over many of us. While in battle we were satisfied with our meagre lot, but now for some reason things have changed. There is no longer a hope for an end coming any moment. And in the R.A.Ch.D. their hierarchy are showing up in a poor light, no idea has been given as to when we are likely to be released, nor are we allowed to make plans with the Home Church; if we could be told when we are likely to be released it would certainly help matters.

But there is something else that has welled up in my mind since the battling days - that one is able to make plans for the future of the men with whom one is working. Two things have come to my mind recently, one a circular letter to be written to all those quarters when demobilised, [so that] the link between all this and the future years will not be broken.

There is in each company or battalion a faithful band of men who are faithful at the Eucharist and other services; these can be a powerful instrument in the Church and [should] not go to seed, they must be brought into the great campaign that has to be waged in the years to come. I am toying with the idea of a Legion and considering the title of 'The Legion of Liberation' - 'The Legion of the Church'; the former seems a more apt title. I have visions of that being a great power in every parish - a cell.

We have now left Schuldehausen and [are] now in a small village called Freckenhorst about fifteen miles from Münster. It is a strong R.C. commune, a beautiful Church of over 900 years old - I am using a small Chapel which was used as a library, but it is over 1,000 years old, and was once the old Church. Above the Altar is either an original or a copy by Reubens of the descent from the Cross, it is beautifully done. At the back of the Chapel is a Cross in wood, with coloured pieces of wood, which represent precious jewels, and coming at the back of it are spiked pieces of wood. This is a replica of the actual Cross in one of the Cathedrals in Moscow, which is very costly, and legend has it that it was dropped by the angels.

I have found the R.C.'s most helpful and they went to a great deal of trouble to prepare the Altar for me.

The Choir that I have started is going extremely well, and the twenty members are extremely keen, we now sing the Canticles etc. and everyone is most helpful.

On **June 6th** we had a holiday, being the anniversary of 'D' Day, a very quiet day. I had a Holy Communion Service in the morning which was quite well attended.

Return 20 Years Later

Margaret saw me off from Victoria Station at 9.30 for Gatwick; while there I met a number of officers of 3rd Br. Inf. Div., General Urquhart, Brig Cass, who commanded 8 Bde. We had coffee with some of the top Brass of 'D' Day. I left by air on B.E.A.[16] and was there joined by Air Marshals, Admirals, and top Generals. On arrival at Deauville I soon found out I was not meant to be on that plane, or the coach that met us, but no-one minded.

[*Unfortunately, there are no more entries in the Diary*].

---

[16] *British European Airways.*

Army Form W.3121
Date recommendation passed forward **1313**

	Received	Passed
Schedule	—	5 July 45 / 15 July 45 / 31 July 45
Brigade	3 July 45	
Division	7 July 45	
Corps	16 July 45	
Army		

Brigade: 3 Br Inf Division: 1 Corps: (N.E.)
Schedule No. ....
Unit: RAChD attd 3 Recce Regt (N.F.)
Rank and Army or Personal No: C.F. IV Class 98071 RAChD
Name: FOX, Benjamin George Burton

Action for which commended (Date and place of action must be stated)	Recommended by	Honour or Reward	(To be left blank)
The Rev B.G.B. Fox, C.F., Chaplain attached to 3rd Recce Reconnaissance Regiment (N.F.) landed with his Regt in June 1944. Throughout the Campaign Padre Fox has been absolutely tireless in his efforts for the welfare of the men. His frequent visits to the forward troops, often under heavy fire, has enabled him to keep himself fully acquainted with all their problems. He has held voluntary church services under every type of condition and has never failed to answer the call of an outlying section or troop. On many occasions during the battle when A.F.V's have been burned, Padre Fox has done far more than the normal duties of a Chaplain in order that the dead crews might have a proper burial. By his magnificent example and his great understanding Padre Fox has earned for himself a position of great esteem among all ranks of his Regiment.	[signed] Comd 3 Recce Regt (N.F.) [signed] Lt Gen. Comd 3rd Br Inf Div [signed] Lieut Gen Comd 1 Corps District	M.B.E. *10PP* [signed] M.C. [signed] M.C. 46/66	P.A. Nil P.A. Nil 12.11.45 P.T.O.

RECOMMENDATION LEADING TO THE AWARD OF THE MILITARY CROSS

MILITARY CROSS   TERRITORIAL DECORATION

3 RECCE REGT.(N.F.),
HOME FORCES.
6.6.44.

My darling Elizabeth,

I want you to regard this letter as a very special one, the reason I write it, is that there is always the possibility I may not return, for modern warfare carries with it so many hazards.

I am writing this in my office just before we embark for the continent, to undertake the greatest movement of tanks that the world has seen, or likely to witness. The events of June 1944 will go down in the

GEORGE'S LETTER TO ELIZABETH - PAGE 1

3 RECCE REGT. (N.F.),
HOME FORCES.

annals of history, you will read about it all at school - it was England's greatest hour.

I am not in the least worried about leaving, for the men will want me more than ever. I am ready both physically and spiritually to meet the hardships that lie in our path. In June 1940 nearly four years ago I left France, a country that was then torn by modern warfare, and left bleeding to be ravaged by a barbaric nation. Whatever the loss may be in men,

3 RECCE REGT.(N.F.),
HOME FORCES.

in this battle, if many do not return, I pray that this war may bring peace to the rest of your life, & never to raise its ugly head again.

I thank God, that I have seen you, and I long for the day when I shall return so that we can be together again.

My darling you will find this world a beautiful place, you will meet people both good & bad — remember the good are in the majority, & the latter, well, do not judge them until you have understood something of their background. You will find

3 RECCE REGT. (N.F.),
HOME FORCES.

there are many who are carrying a Cross, & their chances in life have not always been so numerous as yours.

One thing do not neglect your Church, from its great Sacraments you will find strength for the battle of life, and that Divine Society is the only instrument that can recreate the world.

My darling in closing I leave your dear mother in your care, look after her, for she is very precious to me, let her ideals be yours, & you will then not stray very far.

3 RECCE REGT. (N.F.),
HOME FORCES.

There are some famous words I want to pass on to you - do not forget them, they were said many years ago, by St. Augustine. Write them down in order to remember them, let them be your Guide through life:-

To my fellow-men — A Heart of Love
To my God — A Heart of Flame
To myself — A Heart of Steel.

Good-night darling, follow the best you know, and influence the world in which you live.

If I should not return to you again, I know that I shall be near

3 RECCE REGT. (N.F.),
HOME FORCES.

to you both — and one day we shall meet, and share one another's happiness. Think once was ours.

My love & prayers will be with you both as I cross to the Other Side.

All my love — till we meet again from your loving.

Daddy. xx

ACKNOWLEDGEMENTS

I would like to thank Mrs. Lindsay Mason who helped translate, and who typed my father's hieroglyphics; Colonel Alexander Deuchar for fine-tuning the first draft; and Major General Dare Wilson for his kind and thoughtful Foreword.

I would also like to thank my eldest sister Elizabeth for allowing me to produce the letter which my father wrote to her on 6th June 1994, and her husband Professor Anthony Mellows, for his help with the preparation of the book, including tracing in the Public Record Office the recommendation which led to the award of the Military Cross to my father.

My special thanks must go to Lord and Lady Holderness for printing the book. This is particularly fitting because Lord Holderness became Honorary Colonel of the Queen's Royal Rifles when my father had just finished being its Chaplain and he records that the first job he had was to tackle the War Office to try to extend this. Alas, he failed. I myself followed in my father's footsteps when I became the Territorial Army Chaplain to the 4th (Volunteer) Battalion of the Royal Green Jackets during the time Richard Holderness was still Honorary Colonel.

In addition, I would also like to thank the many friends of the family to whom I have shown the diary for their encouragement to publish it.

The copy of the recommendation for the award, which is Crown copyright, is reproduced by permission of the Controller of Her Majesty's Stationery Office. The map at page 6 and the statement by Field Marshal Viscount Montgomery which is reproduced on the back of the cover are taken from *Assault Division* by Norman Scarfe, 1947.

Colin Fox

INDEX

Argentan 21
Arnhem 27

Bakel 20
Bassum 52
Baustrift 54
Bayeux 16
Beauvais 23
Beaux d'Arts 39
Beethoven 39
Beffelt 31
Bellairs, Miss Sybil 20
Binyon, Laurence 20
Bocage - Louviers 21
Bremen 51,55
Brinkum 54
British European Airways 60
British Liberation Army 41
Brussels 24,31,38-39

Caen 11,13
Caen University 20
Calais 39
Carden Lloyds 16
Cass, Brigadier 60
Caumont 15-16
Chapel of St. George 57
Chardun Cordonnière 19
Cherbourg Peninsular 16
Churchill tanks 43
Claridges Hotel 39
Colleville 15-16
Colombelles 13
Connaught, Duke of, Barracks 40

Deauville 60
Delmenhorst 56-57
Deurne 37

Dingo 46
Divisions - 3rd Br. Infantry 48,52,60
   15 Div. 42
   15 Scottish 38
   16 American Airborne 48
   51 Div. 42
   53 Div. 42
Dodds, Sgt. 33
Dominican Order 30
Dorplein 27
Dorsten 43
Dover 39-40
Dulmen 46
Dvorak 39

Elbe 50
Emmerich 38
Enschede 48
Epron 12
Escaut Canal 25-26
Escotival-Luc-sur-Mer 15
Escoville 14
Estringen 50

Favien, Monsieur 16
Flers 19
Forêt l'Evêque 16
Fox, The Revd. Colin 1
Fox, Catherine (Lemon, Mrs. J.) 2
Fox, Elizabeth
   (Mellows, Mrs. A.R.) 2,17,34
Fox, The Hon: Mrs.
   (Hon. Margaret Davidson)
   1,17,34,39,52,60
Fox, Penelope (Marland, Mrs. J.H.) 2
Fox, Rosemary (Swiney, Mrs. M.) 2
Freckenhorst 58

Gaskell, Peter 19
Gayelle 10
Gelden 42
Goebbels, Josef 54
Gordhuoe 49
Gravenie 18
Grays, Essex 7
Greven 48
Guards Armoured Brigade 42-43, 46, 48

Haltern 44-45
Hamant 26
Handel 34
Haps 29-31
Harbottle, Sgt. 33
Heiligenloh 51
Helmond 27-30
Hospital, 84th General 53
Housman, A.E. 41
Hughes, Rev: F.Ll, D.C.G. 31
Hugo, Monsieur 25

Jean qui Rit, Rest Home 16

Kirchseelte 53
Klosterseelte 53

Lalo 39
Le Bény Bocage 16
La Bijude 12
Legion of Liberation 58
Legion of the Church 58
Les Andelys 22-23
Les Gaillard, Château 22
Levern 51
Lille 39
Lingen 49
Lippramsdorf 44
Lloyd, The Ven, D.A.A.G 49
Louvain 24, 38

Louviers 21

Maas 38
Machenstadt 54
Mathysiend 29
Merriman, Col. Hugh 1
Meuse 30, 37
Midbuul 26
Moselle 41
Motor Church 21
Münster 46, 48, 54, 58

Nelson, H.M.S 8
Newman, Cardinal J.H 24
Nienberge 47-48
Nijmegen 27-28
Nordhorn 49
Normandy Bridgehead 41, 52
Notre Dame, Cathedral of 23
Nottuln 46

Opie, Tpr. 19
Oploo 33-34
Osnabrück 51.57
Ouistream 13
Overloon 31, 36

Pas de Calais 23
Patton, General George 41
Peer 24-25
Periers-sur-le-Dan 10
Purkiss, Bill 53

Rasworthy, Sgt. 44
Rayer, Major 48
Regiments - Bedfordshire & Hertfordshire
 Yeomanry 2
 East Yorks 32
 3rd Reconnaissance (formerly 8th
  Bn Royal Northumberland Fusiliers)
  'The Eight' 1

Regiments (continued) -
   Queens Royal Rifles 2
   5th Royal Inniskilling Dragoon
      Guards 1
   17th Regt. Royal Engineers
      13,38,55
   Royal Ulster Rifles 56
   Warwickshire Regt. 12
Reichwald 38
Rembrandt 25
Reubens 25,59
Rheine 51
Rheims 1
Rhine 27,41-43
Rodney, H.M.S. 12
Roxel 47
Royal Army Chaplains Department 58
Royal Engineers 13
Royal Ulster Rifles 56
Ruhr 50

St. Agatha's Monastery 30
St. Albans Diocese,
     Youth Organiser 52
St. Aulin 15
St. George Chaplain Club 31
St. George and the Dragon,
     Services Club 57
St. Josef's Monastery 35
St. Nazaire 1
St. Paul 21
Saussay de la Campagne 23
Schermbeck 43
Schieldhern 57
Schuldehausen 58
Second Army 15
Seine 22
Shaw, George Bernard 31
Siegfried 41

Sognies 24
Someren 28
Somme 24
Special Service Brigade 42
Stevensbeck 38

Tilbury 7
Tinchebrai 19
Twistingen 52

Urquhart, General 60

Venray 32,36
Vienna 50
Vire 17-19
Vosten Hostie 25

Waal 27
Warspite, H.M.S. 12
Watford 40
Welbeck 42
Wesel 42-43
Wiles, Rev: D.A.C.G., 8th Corps 20